BASIC
JUJITSU
HANDBOOK

Fred Neff's Self-Defense Library

BASIC
JUJITSU
HANDBOOK

Fred Neff

Photographs by James E. Reid

Lerner Publications Company
Minneapolis

The models photographed in this book are Mike Podolinsky, Bruce Bottomley, Bill Polta, Laura Phillips, Rick Rowell, and Jack Engelhart.

LIBRARY OF CONGRESS CATALOGING IN PUBLICATION DATA

Neff, Fred.
Basic jujitsu handbook.

(Fred Neff's Self-Defense Library)
Includes index.
SUMMARY: Text and photographs provide a guide to the basic blocks, punches, kicks, locks, and throws of judo. Includes warm-up exercises.

1. Judo. [1. Judo] I. Reid, James E. II. Title.

GV1114.N44 1976   796.8'152   75-38472
ISBN 0-8225-1151-7

Manufactured in the United States of America

International Standard Book Number: 0-8225-1151-7
Library of Congress Catalog Card Number: 75-38472

5 6 7 8 9 10 90 89 88 87

CONTENTS

*To Mrs. Lena Neff, who has devoted
a lifetime to helping other people*

PREFACE

When I became a student of karate in the 1950's, few Americans had knowledge of the Oriental fighting arts or were interested in learning them. Since that time, however, public interest in the subject has grown considerably. Today, thousands of people all over the country are studying the various fighting arts and are learning that they offer many physical, psychological, and social benefits.

This new interest and involvement in the Oriental fighting arts has created a need for books that can be used as instructional guides for beginning students. FRED NEFF'S SELF-DEFENSE LIBRARY was written to help meet that need. My purpose in writing the series was to provide a basic comprehensive course on self-defense, based on the major Oriental disciplines of karate, judo, and jujitsu. In preparing each book, I was careful to include not only the physical techniques of Oriental fighting but also the underlying philosophical principles. This is important because an understanding of both elements is required of every martial arts student. Finally, in selecting the particular self-defense techniques for each book, I tried to include techniques that could be of practical use to the average person and that could be performed effectively and safely through practice. I genuinely hope that each and every reader of the SELF-DEFENSE LIBRARY benefits as much as I have from studying the martial arts.

I would like to express my thanks and appreciation to Mr. Harry Lerner, president of Lerner Publications Company, for his enthusiasm and support in the development of this series. I would also like to thank my students, who contributed their time and skill to demonstrating the various fighting techniques in the books. Finally, I would like to express special appreciation to the staff at Lerner Publications for its work in the production of the series.

Fred Neff

INTRODUCTION

Jujitsu is an ancient Oriental art of self-defense and counterattack. People who practice jujitsu rely on a series of skillful body movements to block an attack or to end a fight quickly.

The word *jujitsu* means "gentle art." This is an appropriate name, because jujitsu techniques are basically defensive rather than aggressive. A jujitsu person never attacks: he or she always allows an attacker to make the first aggressive move. The jujitsu person blocks the attack and watches for the exact moment when the aggressor leaves himself or herself open to counterattack. Then, if necessary, the jujitsu person ends the fight quickly with a well-aimed punch or kick, or uses a holding technique to contain the attacker. In some cases, the jujitsu person may end the fight by throwing the attacker. With proper throwing techniques, a skilled jujitsu person can often stop a stronger, heavier opponent. Thus, jujitsu is a self-defense method that depends on skill and judgment rather than on sheer physical strength.

When a person studies jujitsu, he or she learns not only the physical techniques but a philosophy as well. This philosophy stresses self-control, and it encourages an attitude of kindness and respect for all living creatures.

HISTORY OF JUJITSU

Both the philosophy and the techniques of jujitsu are very ancient — so ancient, in fact, that historians do not know exactly how and where they were first developed. Many authorities think that these non-aggressive techniques were invented by Buddhist monks in ancient India or China. The monks, in turn, may have taught jujitsu skills to the common people, who were forbidden by law to carry weapons.

Although the origins of jujitsu are uncertain, the gentle art was most fully developed by the Japanese. Between the 12th and 17th centuries, jujitsu was used by Japanese warriors, called *samurai*. The samurai used jujitsu skills for close-in fighting when they lost their swords or spears in battle. As time passed, the warriors developed hundreds of different jujitsu systems. Although these systems were based on a variety of techniques, they all shared one philosophy — that of *Bushido*, or the "Way of the Warrior." The Bushido philosophy emphasized courtesy, self-improvement, and kindness toward other people.

The samurai continued to practice both the philosophy and the fighting techniques of jujitsu until the middle of the 19th century. At this point, the modern age of guns and war machinery had begun, and people no longer fought in hand-to-hand combat. So the samurai way of fighting gradually died out.

Jujitsu techniques were kept alive, however, by a few dedicated students of the gentle art. After World War II, interest in jujitsu spread to Western countries, where people recognized that the techniques were a very effective means of self-defense. Today, thousands of people all over the world practice both the philosophy and the fighting techniques of this ancient art.

COMMON QUESTIONS ABOUT JUJITSU

Beginning jujitsu students are always curious about the non-aggressive aspects of the gentle art. In this chapter are seven commonly asked questions about situations in which jujitsu may be used. You are encouraged to read the answers to these questions carefully, because they help to explain the underlying philosophy of jujitsu. Once you understand the philosophy, you will be better able to judge when and how to apply jujitsu techniques.

1. When should I use my jujitsu training?

Since jujitsu techniques are basically defensive, you should use them only when you are in immediate danger of being physically harmed. You should never use the techniques to start a fight. In fact, the philosophy of the gentle art teaches that a person should try to avoid a fight whenever possible. As a jujitsu student, you must learn to control your temper, and to ignore threats, insults, and verbal challenges. Because knowledge of jujitsu gives you a physical advantage over other people, you have a responsibility to practice self-control at all times.

There are times, however, when a fight may be unavoidable. If a person actually makes a move to attack you, then you will be forced to defend yourself. But you must always wait until the aggressor makes the first move before you respond with any jujitsu technique.

2. Is there a practical reason for waiting until an attacker makes the first move?

As you have seen, there are important philosophical reasons for allowing an attacker to make the first move. But there are practical reasons, too. Through experience, jujitsu people know that an attacker almost always leaves a sensitive part of his or her body open to counterattack when making an aggressive move. By waiting for this to happen, a jujitsu person can quickly end the fight with an appropriate hold, punch, or kick. Sometimes, too, an aggressor will become off-balanced while moving to attack. This makes it possible for the jujitsu person to throw the attacker.

3. Must I wait until I am actually hit or thrown before I offer resistance to an attacker?

It is not necessary for you to wait until you are struck or thrown before using self-defense tactics. It is true that you must let the attacker make the first aggressive move. An aggressive move, however, may be defined as any physical movement that shows aggressive intent. For example, when someone grabs your arm or raises a hand to strike you, that person has probably shown an intent to hurt you. You may then defend yourself with the appropriate jujitsu technique.

4. How do I develop enough self-confidence to stand up to an attacker?

Jujitsu is an excellent and effective art of self-defense. If you have thoroughly learned and practiced the fighting techniques, you should have faith in your ability to defend yourself against any attacker. Jujitsu teaches that believing you can do something will actually help you to do it.

5. Should I let people know that I have studied jujitsu, so that they will respect me and will think twice about picking a fight?

A jujitsu student should never brag or talk about the skill that he or she may have acquired in fighting. According to the principles of the gentle art, a person should earn respect by behaving kindly toward people. You should therefore concentrate on getting along well with people, as well as on developing fighting skills. You will find that it is much more satisfying to be respected for your good deeds than it is to be feared for your fighting abilities.

6. Can I learn jujitsu techniques by watching television and movies?

It is not a good idea to copy self-defense techniques that are performed in television and movie dramas. These techniques are staged to look exciting — not to show the way in which they should really be done.

7. How long will it take me to become an expert in jujitsu?

It takes many years of hard work to become a jujitsu expert. There are no shortcuts in the learning process: each technique must be perfected through constant practice. If you are sincerely interested in learning jujitsu, you should take classes from a qualified instructor who can teach you both the correct techniques and the philosophy of the gentle art. Although reading books about jujitsu will acquaint you with the basic principles, you can master the techniques only through time, effort, and constant practice.

1.

LIMBERING AND STRETCHING EXERCISES

Before you can perform jujitsu techniques, your body must be in good condition. If your body is strong and flexible, you will not strain your muscles when you block, punch, kick, or throw. The exercises in this chapter are designed to condition the muscle groups that are used in doing the various jujitsu techniques. It is recommended that you do all of these exercises before each practice session.

NOTE: Practice all exercises slowly at first. By doing a little stretching each day, you can limber up gradually without injuring your muscles.

Front Bending Exercise

Stand straight with your legs slightly apart. Without bending your knees, reach down and touch the ground with the palms of your hands.

Body Twisting Exercise

Stand with your legs apart and your knees slightly bent, and extend your arms straight out to either side. Twist your body at the waist as far to the right as you can. Then twist to the left.

Leg Stretching Exercise

Stand in an upright, relaxed position with your feet together. Without bending your knees, kick one leg, and then the other, straight up in front of you. Try to kick as high as possible.

Basic Flexibility Exercise

Stand in an upright, relaxed position, and slowly spread your legs as far apart as possible.

NOTE: At first, stretch your legs only as far as they will go without strain. If you do a little stretching each day, you will eventually be able to ease yourself all the way to the ground.

2.

BASIC BODY MECHANICS AND SENSITIVE AREAS

In jujitsu, both the hands and the feet are used for self-defense. However, only certain areas of the hands and feet should actually make contact with an opponent's body when you deliver a punch or a kick. This chapter explains how to position your hands and feet so that the appropriate areas are used for striking.

In addition to learning these positions, you must also learn what parts of an opponent's body to aim for when you punch or kick. There are certain parts of the body, such as nerve centers, that are especially sensitive to attack. If you direct a blow at one of these sensitive areas, you can stop even a strong attacker immediately. This chapter includes two charts that show which parts of the body are considered proper striking areas for jujitsu.

HAND POSITIONS FOR STRIKING
The Closed Fist

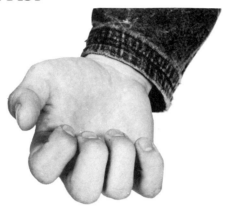

To make a proper closed fist, fold your fingers tightly into your palm and place your thumb across your forefinger and middle finger.

The first and second knuckles of your fist should make contact with your target.

The closed fist can be used to strike an aggressor's head, chest, or stomach.

The Open Hand

Stiffen the open fingers of your hand and bend the tips slightly forward. Fold your thumb down so that it rests next to the palm of your hand. The outside edge of your hand should make contact with your target. The open hand can be used to strike an aggressor's ribs, neck, or head.

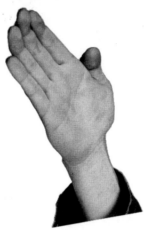

FOOT POSITIONS FOR KICKING

Kicks Using the Ball of the Foot

The part of the foot that is used for kicking is the ball, which is the fleshy ridge at the base of the toes. When you use the ball of your foot to strike an attacker, be sure to turn your toes upward so that they are not injured.

The front kick, described in Chapter 6, makes use of the ball of the foot to strike an attacker's groin, chest, or head.

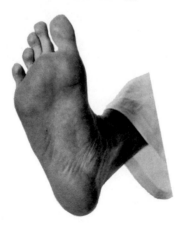

Kicks Using the Heel of the Foot

Another part of the foot that is used for kicking is the heel. The side kick and the back kick, described in Chapter 6, make use of the heel to strike an attacker's head, chest, or groin. When kicking with your heel, remember to turn your toes upward in order to avoid injuring them.

Chart of Sensitive Areas

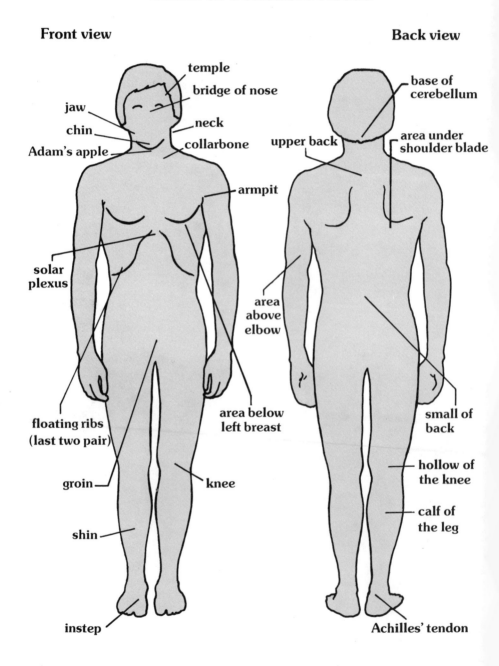

Front view

Back view

temple
bridge of nose
jaw
chin
neck
Adam's apple
collarbone
armpit
solar plexus
floating ribs (last two pair)
groin
knee
area below left breast
shin
instep

base of cerebellum
upper back
area under shoulder blade
area above elbow
small of back
hollow of the knee
calf of the leg
Achilles' tendon

3.

FIGHTING STANCES

Fighting stances are special standing positions from which the various blocks, punches, and kicks are performed. These stances are essential to the art of jujitsu. They not only help to build strength and flexibility in the legs, but they also give the body stability in a fight. If your fighting stances are strong and stable, you will not be easily thrown off balance by an attacker, and your counterattacks will be strong as well. In order to develop a strong stance, you must practice two important principles of jujitsu.

The first principle is that of *inner strength*. Inner strength is both an awareness of your own inner power and an ability to control that power. To achieve inner strength, you must concentrate, or focus your thoughts, on your lower stomach area, where your power is centered. This concentration will result in a stance that is very difficult for an aggressor to break.

Proper breathing will help you to use your inner strength to its fullest advantage. When you make a defensive move, such as a block or punch, bring air up from your lower stomach area and sharply exhale it through your nose and mouth. This action will distribute your power throughout your body. In this way, your inner strength will add power to all of your movements.

Another important jujitsu principle involves the use of power in your hips. When you counterattack, twist or turn your hip in the direction of your attack. This twisting will allow you to throw your body weight into the attack and will thus make your movements very powerful.

Keep these two principles—inner strength and hip power—in mind when you practice the fighting stances described in this chapter. It is helpful to practice the various stances in front of a mirror, so that you can compare your body positions with those shown in the photographs. When you feel you have mastered the individual stances, practice moving quickly and smoothly from one stance to another.

The Horse Stance

The horse stance is one of the most commonly used stances in jujitsu. It is very versatile and can be used for making any kind of counterattack. This stance allows you a great deal of flexibility, because you can easily move from it into either of the other stances.

Learning Steps

1. Spread your feet apart and bend your knees, much as you would if you were riding a horse. Your toes should point slightly inward.

2. Make fists of both hands and place your fists, palms up, at waist level.*

3. The upper half of your body should remain erect, and your weight should be distributed evenly between both legs.

*NOTE: There are many ways to hold the hands in the various fighting stances. But generally it is best to keep both hands at waist level, with at least one of them in a fist.

The Modified Horse Stance

The modified horse stance can be used either for defensive moves or for counterattacks. Almost all of the blocks, kicks, and punches in jujitsu can be performed from this stance.

Learning Steps

1. Spread your feet apart as in the horse stance, but place one foot slightly in front of the other, so that you are not facing your attacker straight on.

2. Make one hand into a fist and hold it, palm up, at waist level. Leave the other hand open and hold it in front of your body, palm down.*

3. Your knees should be bent slightly, and your body weight should be evenly distributed between both legs.

*NOTE: The hand that is in front of your body may sometimes be made into a fist. There is also an alternative way to hold the hands in which both hands are made into fists and held, palms up, at waist level.

The Back Stance

The back stance should be used primarily for defending yourself from a series of strong punches or kicks. When you are in this stance your body will be very stable, and it will be difficult for an aggressor to knock you over.

Learning Steps

1. Place one leg in front of the other so that the distance between your feet is about twice the width of your shoulders.

2. Your back leg should be sharply bent, with the foot pointing to the side, and should carry about 70 percent of your body weight. Your front leg should be only slightly bent, with the foot pointed forward.

3. Make one hand into a fist and place it at your hip. Leave your other hand open and hold it like a shield just in front of your body.

MOVEMENT FROM THE FIGHTING STANCES

Jujitsu teaches that a person should be physically well balanced when moving, as well as when standing still. In order to maintain your balance while moving, you must learn to slide your feet as you step. If you slide, your body will always be in a stable position for performing a block, punch, kick, or throw. Body stability will also make you less vulnerable to attack, because an aggressor will find it difficult to throw you off balance.

The Single-Foot Sliding Step

Sliding is useful for covering short distances quickly. You can use the single-foot sliding step to move forward or backward from any of the fighting stances.

Learning Steps

1. Starting from a standing position, simply slide one foot forward. (To move backward, slide one foot to the rear.)

2. Make sure that you maintain proper balance as you slide, and that the upper part of your body remains erect.

The Double-Foot Sliding Step

This technique allows you to move forward while keeping the same foot in front of you at all times. It can be done from any of the fighting stances. If you wish to do this technique from the horse stance, however, you must first do a single foot slide in order to get one foot out in front of the other.

Learning Steps

1. Starting from a standing position, slide your front foot forward.

2. Slide your back foot along behind, maintaining the original distance between your two feet. Be sure to maintain proper balance as you slide.

NOTE: To move backward, slide your back foot to the rear, and follow with your front foot.

4.

BLOCKING TECHNIQUES

In many fighting situations, your first concern will be to avoid an attacker's initial punch or kick. You can use the blocking techniques in this chapter to protect yourself from an aggressor until you find an opportunity to counterattack. All of these techniques can be performed from any of the fighting stances.

It is best to practice blocking with a fellow jujitsu student. If you do not have a partner, however, you can practice in front of a mirror and imagine that an attacker is throwing a punch or kick at you. When you practice, keep the following points in mind.

1. Before you perform any block, determine exactly where you want your block to meet the aggressor's arm or leg. Then focus your eyes on that point. If you focus on your target, your block will be accurate and very powerful.

2. Practice all techniques slowly at the beginning of each practice session. Then do them at medium speed, and finally at a fast speed. Do not speed up, however, until you are sure that you have mastered the proper form.

BLOCKING ATTACKS TO THE LOWER BODY
The Downward Block
The downward block is very useful for blocking punches or kicks aimed at the lower stomach and the groin. This block can be performed from any of the fighting stances.

Learning Steps
1. Starting from one of the basic stances, place the fist of your blocking arm next to your ear. Keep the other fist at your waist, ready to counterpunch.

2. Swing your blocking arm downward, so that the outside edge of your forearm stops the attacker's punch or kick. Your arm should be fully extended when it meets the attacker's leg or arm.

The Low Cross Block

This cross block is especially useful for stopping kicks to the lower areas of the body, such as the stomach or groin. It can be performed from any of the fighting stances.

Learning Steps

1. Begin from one of the basic stances. Here, the modified horse stance is shown.

2. Make fists of both hands, and cross your wrists in front of the lower part of your body to stop the attacker's kicking leg.

3. While performing this block you may bend from the knees, but try to keep the upper part of your body as erect as possible.

BLOCKING ATTACKS TO THE MIDDLE OF THE BODY

The Forearm Block

This powerful block is used primarily against punching attacks to the chest and stomach. It is most effective if done from a stance (such as the modified horse stance) in which one arm is already positioned in front of the body.

Learning Steps

1. Start from the modified horse stance. The arm that is held in front of your body will be your blocking arm. Your other hand should rest at your hip, ready to throw a counterpunch after you have blocked the attacker's arm.

2. With a strong, snapping motion, bring your blocking arm up from its lowered position so that the inside edge of your forearm meets the attacker's punching arm. Keep your blocking arm sharply bent in order to withstand the force of the attacker's blow.

BLOCKING ATTACKS TO THE UPPER BODY

The Rising Block

The rising block is most often used as a defense against punching attacks to the head and chest. Like the forearm block, this block is best performed from a stance in which one arm is held out in front of the body.

Learning Steps

1. Start from a modified horse stance. The hand of your blocking arm (the arm that is in front of your body) should be made into a fist. Your other fist should rest at your waist, ready to counterattack.

2. Swing your blocking arm up in front of your head, and twist it so that the soft part of your forearm faces the attacker. Keep your arm sharply bent in order to withstand the attacker's blow.

The Upward Cross Block

This block is most useful for stopping punches aimed at the head. It can be done from any of the fighting stances.

Learning Steps

1. Begin in one of the basic stances. Here, the modified horse stance is shown.

2. Keeping both hands open, bring them up so that the wrists are crossed when they reach the level of your head. Your hands should be kept open so that you can grasp the attacker's punching arm after you have stopped it.

3. This block will be most powerful if your elbows are kept close to your body.

5.
HAND TECHNIQUES

The two basic types of hand techniques—punches and strikes—are excellent methods for counterattacking after you have blocked an aggressor's first move. Each of these techniques gets its power from a particular kind of arm movement. A punch involves a thrusting motion. When you punch, power moves from the shoulder of your punching arm down into your hand. A strike, however, gets its power from a snapping motion in the elbow of the striking arm.

This chapter describes basic techniques for punching or striking an opponent. Each technique has a specific form that you must learn in order to gain the power you need for an effective counterattack. The three principles listed below will also help you to develop powerful hand techniques.

1. Before you deliver a blow, focus your eyes on the spot you are attempting to hit. If you focus on your target, your blow will be more accurate.

2. Practice inner strength techniques in order to gain power for your punches and strikes. Remember to exhale as you deliver your blow.

3. Always thrust your hip in the direction of your counterattack. This will make your blow very powerful.

The Forefist Punch

The forefist punch is a very powerful technique that can be performed from any of the fighting stances. It can be used to hit an attacker's chest or head. As this punch is thrown, the fist is twisted to give more power to the attack.

Learning Steps

1. Begin from one of the basic stances. Hold your punching fist, palm up, just above your hip. Your other hand should be held out in front of you, with fingers open as if you were grabbing something.

2. Thrust your punching hand forward, twisting your fist quickly so that the palm faces the ground and the knuckles point forward. At the same time, pull your other arm back to a waist-level fist position.

NOTE: When you practice with a partner, *never* actually strike or punch the person. Always stop your blow at least two inches (five centimeters) from your partner's head or body.

The Forward-Stepping Forefist Punch

This technique has a great deal of power, because all of the body weight is thrown into the punch. It is used to hit the upper part of an opponent's body (usually the head or chest), and is best performed from the modified horse stance.

Learning Steps

1. Begin by standing in a modified horse stance.

2. Step forward with your back foot, and as it passes your front foot, throw a forefist punch. Your leg and your fist should move forward at the same time, from the same side of your body.

3. Be sure to turn your hip toward your opponent as you deliver your punch. Your stepping foot should end up in front of your body after the punch is thrown.

The Open-Hand Strike

The open-hand strike is especially useful for hitting an aggressor's neck or ribs. This strike is best performed from the modified horse stance.

Learning Steps

1. Start from the modified horse stance.

2. Bring your striking hand across your body and hold it next to your ear with the palm facing your head. (Use the open-hand position, described in Chapter 2.) Your other hand should be held in front of you, with the palm facing the attacker.

3. Swing your striking hand forward toward your target, twisting your wrist so that your palm faces downward. The outside edge of your hand will then strike the target. As your striking hand moves forward, make a fist of your other hand and bring it back to your hip.

6.
FOOT TECHNIQUES

Kicking techniques are a very powerful means of counter-attack, because the human leg has a great deal of strength. Because of the leg's long reach, a kick can also be performed from a safer distance than can a punch or strike.

The kicking techniques in this chapter may be done from any of the fighting stances. In order to perform these kicks in the most effective way, you should keep the following principles in mind.

1. For an accurate kick, focus your eyes on your target before you begin.

2. Your supporting leg must always be bent slightly and planted firmly on the ground.

3. Always maintain proper balance and stability when kicking.

4. Remember to use your hip power to give your kick greater impact.

The Front Kick

The front kick is a very powerful technique that can be used to strike an aggressor's knees, groin, stomach, or head.

Learning Steps

1. Bend the knee of your kicking leg and lift it toward your chest. Be sure to turn your toes upward so that they are not injured when your foot hits the target.

2. Snap your kicking leg forward from the knee and hit your target with the ball of your foot.

NOTE: If you practice kicking with a partner, you must be especially careful to see that no one is injured. *Never* actually kick your partner—keep your kicking foot *at least* two inches (five centimeters) from your partner's head or body.

The Side Kick

The side kick is a very effective method of counterattack. It can be used to hit an aggressor's knees, groin, stomach, or head.

Learning Steps

1. Bend the knee of your kicking leg and lift it toward your chest. Be sure that your toes are turned upward.

2. Thrust your kicking leg out to the side of your body and hit the target with the heel of your foot.

The Back Kick

The back kick is used to defend against attacks from the rear. In doing this kick, it is especially important to maintain proper balance, so that there is enough power in the kick to stop an aggressor. This kick is best performed from the modified horse stance.

Learning Steps

1. Turn your head so that you can see behind you. At the same time, bend the knee of your kicking leg and bring it up toward your chest, as you would in doing a front kick.

2. Thrust your kicking leg directly behind you, using a snapping motion of the knee. The heel of your foot should hit the target.

7.
FALLING TECHNIQUES

Learning how to fall properly is an essential part of jujitsu training. If you know how to fall correctly, you will be less vulnerable to injury when you are thrown or tripped by an attacker. You will also gain confidence, because you will not fear being thrown. For these reasons, you should constantly practice the falling techniques outlined in this chapter. When you practice falling, keep in mind the following important points.

1. Always do the standard sequence of jujitsu exercises before you begin your falling practice. Your body must be loose and flexible in order to fall properly.

2. Always practice on a large, thick mat in order to protect yourself from injury. A beginning jujitsu student should *never* practice falling on a hard surface.

3. Do each fall slowly at first. This will give you a chance to develop good form. Do not speed up your movements until you have mastered the proper form.

The Side Fall

The side fall is the most commonly used falling technique in jujitsu. It is a very effective means of avoiding injury when you are thrown over an opponent's hip or shoulder. You can also use this fall when you are tripped, or when you are thrown by a leg sweep.

Learning Steps

1. Start in a squatting position, with one leg crossed just in front of the other.

2. Gradually slide your front leg forward. This sliding action should cause you to lose your balance and to fall on your side. As you fall, bring your arm up in the air.

3. Just before you hit the mat, beat the palm of your raised hand against the mat to break your fall.

NOTE: It is important that your body land properly, so that knees, ankles, and other sensitive spots are not injured. Make sure that after you land, your body is in the position illustrated in this photo.

The Back Fall

This fall can be used when you are thrown or tripped so that you fall directly backward.

Learning Steps

1. Begin in a squatting position with your knees deeply bent. Extend your arms directly in front of your body, and tuck in your chin.

2. Allow your body to fall back, raising your arms as you fall. Be sure to keep your chin securely tucked in. This will prevent your head from hitting the mat when you land.

3. Just before your back touches the mat, break your fall by slapping your forearms against the mat about six inches (15 centimeters) from either side of your body.

NOTE: When you have completed the fall, your body should be in the position shown in this photo. Note that the head is completely raised off the mat.

The Front Fall

The front fall is most useful when someone tackles you from behind. You can also use it any time that you slip and fall forward.

Learning Steps

1. Start in a kneeling position on the mat.

2. Rise up and let your body fall forward. Bring your arms up, with palms facing the mat.

3. When you fall, slap the mat with the palms of both hands to break your fall. Your stomach should not touch the mat at any point during the fall.

NOTE: It is very important that your hands and arms remain stationary after they slap the mat. They will support your body and will keep it from hitting the mat.

8.

THROWING TECHNIQUES

Beginning jujitsu students are always fascinated by the idea of throwing an opponent. Students should keep in mind, however, that learning to throw a person takes a lot of skill, hard work, and practice.

Although there are no formal stances from which throws must be done, there *are* specific forms and movements that must be mastered for each kind of throw. You must also learn which throws are best suited to particular kinds of attacks. Every throw must be carefully practiced until the movements become a smooth, almost automatic response to an attack.

To develop correct form in throwing, it is a good idea to begin practicing alone, in front of a mirror. In this way, you can compare your body positions and movements with those shown in the photographs. However, you will also need to practice with a fellow jujitsu student. When you do so, it is very important that you keep in mind the following essential safety rules.

1. Always do the complete sequence of warm-up exercises before each practice session.

2. Always practice on a large, thick safety mat.

3. Never throw anyone who has not mastered the falling techniques, and don't allow yourself to be thrown until you are sure that you know how to fall.

4. Never try to "surprise" your partner—warn him or her before you attempt a throw.

NOTE: If you were to use the throws in this chapter during an actual fight, you would let go of the attacker's arm as he or she fell. But in a practice session, you should maintain your grip on your partner's arm as he or she hits the mat. This helps to prevent injury by forcing your partner to land in a relatively safe position.

OFF-BALANCING AN AGGRESSOR BEFORE THROWING

Before you attempt to throw an aggressor, the aggressor's balance should be broken. This is necessary because an attacker who is off balance will have a difficult time using his or her strength to resist your throw.

Many attackers will break their own balance simply by making the first aggressive move. For example, aggressors who are pushing their opponents backward usually off-balance themselves by putting their weight on the balls of their feet. These aggressors can easily be thrown forward, because their balance is broken in that direction. On the other hand, aggressors who are pulling their opponents forward usually off-balance themselves to the rear and can therefore be thrown backward quite easily.

There are situations, however, when an attacker is not off balance, even though he or she has made an aggressive move. In these cases, you must break the aggressor's balance by pushing or pulling the aggressor before attempting a throw.

As a student of the gentle art, you should spend a lot of time learning to off-balance an aggressor. You can practice on a mat with a fellow jujitsu student. When you practice, keep in mind the following helpful points.

1. Always observe an aggressor's stance carefully before you attempt a throw. The throw should be made at the exact moment when the aggressor is off balance.

2. Keep your body loose and relaxed at all times, so that you can respond quickly when you see that an attacker is off balance.

3. Remember that an aggressor is always easiest to throw in the direction in which he or she is moving.

4. If an aggressor is not off balance, you can break the aggressor's balance by directing his or her energy to your own advantage. If the aggressor pushes, you should pull. If the aggressor pulls, then you should push.

The Big Hip Throw

The big hip throw is one of the most basic throws in jujitsu. It is useful when an attacker is close to you and has a tight grip on your clothing. This throw may also be used effectively when an attacker is trying to push you backward.

Learning Steps

1. Face your attacker and place your right foot next to the inside of his or her right foot. At the same time, put your right arm around the attacker's waist and grab his or her right arm with your left hand.

2. Pivot on your right foot and step back with your left foot. The front of the attacker's body should now be resting against the back of your hip. At this point, your knees should be deeply bent and your toes pointed outward.

3. To execute the throw, spring up from your bent-knee position and pull the attacker forward over your hip.

47

The Shoulder Throw

The shoulder throw is a very powerful defense against an aggressor who is moving forward to attack. It is also an effective technique for a small person to use against a tall aggressor. This is because it is easy for a smaller person to execute one of the key steps of the throw—that of fitting one shoulder under the aggressor's armpit.

Learning Steps

1. Face your attacker and place your right foot in front of his or her right foot. At the same time, grasp your attacker's right arm with your left hand.

2. Pivot on your right foot and step back with your left foot, so that your back is turned toward the aggressor. (It is important that both of your knees be deeply bent when you reach this position.) As you pivot, pull the aggressor's right arm forward, and swing your right arm under the aggressor's armpit. Grab the aggressor by the shoulder with your right hand. Now the aggressor should be on your back, ready to be thrown.

3. To execute the throw, spring up from your bent-knee position, force your hips backward into the aggressor's body, and pull the person forward across your shoulder.

The Big Outside Sweeping Leg Thr

This throw can be used in a situation in which an aggressor i, very close to you and is threatening to attack.

Learning Steps

1. Face the attacker directly. Then step forward, placing your left foot next to the outside of the aggressor's right foot. At the same time, grab the aggressor's right arm with your left hand and pull it downward. With your right hand, push the aggressor's body slightly backward. (If all of these movements have been made correctly, the attacker's balance should be broken to the rear.)

2. Slip your right leg behind the aggressor's right leg, so that the back of your leg presses tightly against the back of the aggressor's leg.

3. To execute the throw, sweep your right leg behind you so that it takes the aggressor's leg out from under him or her.

The Big Inside Sweeping Leg Throw

This is a very effective throw to use when an aggressor is standing close to you with his or her legs spread wide apart.

Learning Steps

1. Grasp the attacker's arms and push slightly backward so that his or her balance is broken to the rear.

2. Twist your right hip forward and place your right leg between the attacker's legs.

3. To execute the throw, continue pushing the attacker backward with your hands, and use the back of your right leg to sweep the attacker's left leg out from under him or her.

The Scooping Throw

This throw can be used in many different self-defense situations. It is especially useful when an attacker has a strong hold on you.

Learning Steps

1. Begin by facing your attacker. Then pivot and swing your body around so that you are standing to the side of the attacker. Place your right foot behind the attacker's right foot, and your left foot to the outside of the attacker's left foot. At this point, both of your knees should be deeply bent.

2. Bring your right arm across the front of the attacker's body and get a firm grip on the back of his or her right leg. At the same time, grab the attacker's left leg with your left arm.

3. To execute the throw, push your hips forward to off-balance the attacker, and lift the attacker's legs off the ground with your hands.

9.

HOLDING TECHNIQUES

Holds are techniques that enable you to contain an attacker—to prevent him or her from making any further aggressive moves. These techniques are useful in many different fighting situations. It is important to remember, however, that holds are not meant to take the place of other jujitsu techniques. Many beginning students want to apply a hold whenever an aggressor is threatening to attack. But these techniques should only be used when an aggressor is close to you, and when the limb to which you are going to apply the hold is not moving. If, for example, an aggressor is throwing a punch at you, you must always stop his or her arm with a block before you apply any hold. Both hand and foot attacks should *always* be blocked before any hold is attempted.

The only proper way to learn holds is to practice them with a fellow jujitsu student until you can do them smoothly and efficiently. It is very important to practice these techniques safely so that no one is injured. Therefore, you should follow the safety rules listed below.

1. Never apply full force to a hold, or push down with a fast, jerky motion.

2. Before practicing, make an agreement with your partner that you will tap one another on the arm or leg if any hold is applied with too much force. When tapped by your partner, you should instantly release any pressure that you are applying to the hold.

The Straight Arm Hold

Learning Steps

1. Grasp the aggressor's lower right arm or wrist with your right hand.

2. Pivot and step to a position behind the aggressor's arm. As you pivot, pull the arm forward and twist it so that the elbow is facing upward.

3. Place your left hand on the aggressor's elbow and push down forcefully.

4. To put added pressure on the aggressor's arm, force the wrist back with your right hand.

The Rear Arm Hold

Learning Steps

1. Grasp the aggressor's right wrist with both of your hands and lift his or her arm straight up.

2. Step underneath the raised arm and pivot on the balls of your feet so that you end up standing directly behind the aggressor.

3. At this point, the aggressor's arm should be bent. Push your left elbow hard against the aggressor's back and pull his or her arm up. Maintain steady upward pressure on the arm.

The Front Wrist Hold

Learning Steps

1. Stand with your feet firmly planted, left foot forward, and grasp the aggressor's right wrist with your right hand.

2. Lift the aggressor's wrist up as you twist his or her arm. The palm of the aggressor's hand should end up facing the aggressor.

3. Now, grip the aggressor's wrist with both of your hands. Take a step forward with your back leg, placing it behind the aggressor's legs, and put your right elbow against the aggressor's chest.

4. Lean forward and to the outside of the aggressor, and push steadily down on his or her wrist.

The Side Wrist Hold

Learning Steps

1. Standing at the aggressor's side, reach across your body and grab the aggressor's right hand with your right hand.

2. Insert your left elbow in the crook of the aggressor's arm. At the same time, pull his or her hand close to your body and twist it so that the palm is facing you and the thumb is pointed toward the ground.

3. Now, press down on the aggressor's wrist with both hands and lean from your hips toward the aggressor's body. Your elbow should remain in the crook of the aggressor's arm, exerting a steady downward pressure.

SAFETY RULES

When you practice jujitsu techniques, you must always take proper safety precautions in order to avoid injury. This is especially important when you are practicing with a partner. You should never treat a practice session as if it were a competitive fighting situation. Remember that it is a time for you and your partner to work together on improving your skills.

Listed below are six basic safety rules. If you and your partner follow these rules, you can reduce the likelihood of injury during practice sessions.

1. Always do all of the warm-up exercises before each practice session, so that your body will be strong and flexible.

2. Never try to "surprise" your partner during practice—always warn him or her before you attempt to perform any technique.

3. Never actually hit your partner when you practice punches, strikes, or kicks. Always stop your blow *at least* two inches (five centimeters) from your partner's head or body.

4. Always practice falls and throws on a large, thick safety mat—never on a hard surface.

5. Practice throwing *only* when you and your partner are sure that you both know how to fall properly.

6. When practicing holding techniques, do not apply full force to any hold. Work out a "warning system" with your partner whereby you agree to signal each other if a hold begins to cause discomfort.

INDEX

ABOUT THE AUTHOR

Fred Neff has been a student of the Asian fighting arts for most of his life. He started his training at the age of eight and eventually specialized in karate. Today Mr. Neff holds the rank of fifth degree black belt in that fighting art. In addition to karate, he is also proficient in judo and jujitsu. For many years, Mr. Neff has used his knowledge of the Asian fighting arts to educate others. He has taught karate at the University of Minnesota, the University of Wisconsin, and Hamline University and Inver Hills College in St. Paul, Minnesota. He has also organized and supervised self-defense classes in public schools, private schools, and in city recreation departments. Included in his teaching program have been classes for law enforcement officers.

Fred Neff graduated with high distinction from the University of Minnesota College of Education in 1970. In 1976, he received his J.D. degree from William Mitchell College of Law in St. Paul, Minnesota. Mr. Neff is now a practicing attorney in Minneapolis, Minnesota.